Online Reputation Management

25 Things You Need to Know

By Jim Hayne

Table of Contents

About the Author

Jim Hayne is an American business marketing and sales specialist. He lives in La Verne, California which is 40 miles east of Los Angeles.

Jim Has had three main careers in his life. First, he had the opportunity to minister to young people as a youth minister for both Presbyterian and Baptist churches located mostly in Southern California. Jim did this for over eighteen and a half years (you can tell he worked with youth when he emphasises the half year) before making a change to a new career in wealth management. Working as a wealth manager, Jim helped both families and small business investors plan and invest toward their desired goals. After seventeen plus years helping individuals with their money, Jim has helped many companies as a sales and marketing specialist. Jim main focus is to move the needle in a positive direction for any person he works with.

Working in the wealth management arena, Jim was constantly approached by many so-called advertising specialist claiming they were the experts in delivering leads and he would have great success, if only he would invest in their system providing quality leads. One after another of these so called amazing lead systems failed miserably, and often delivered little or no results at all.   Realizing that success was really about getting new paying customers and clients through his door,   Jim began to grow his business by studying advertising and marketing and creating his own marketing of his design system. Realizing that the old adage of sharpening the saw before cutting a tree really was important.

One thing you learn as a youth minister is that you do not wait for the young people to show up at the church, but you must visit the places the youth are located and build relationships there. When Jim realized the solution to build his business was already answered in what he had been doing for almost two decades that put together a solution that worked.

Today, principals are the same, but methods may be a bit different due to technology. Regular mail and postcards through the post office has been substituted by email. Although mailings may have its usefulness because its stands out since so many do not use this method anymore. Seminars have been replaced with webinars, and door knocking has been replaced with Facebook and other social media platforms.

Asking for referrals from friends have even been supplanted by Google, Yelp and Facebook and other online platforms. Why the change? Simple, we can save time and get more feedback by looking at the reviews scores and even dig deeper and read the reviews themselves.

The internet has changed the way we interact with one another and with our shopping. Not all of the change is good, but most would agree it is the preferred method to interact with one another. When we realize that currently Google is the number one source for research on just about anything, we know that Google is not going away anytime soon. Most Americans use Google to find suggestions and recommendations for the services and products they desire. Getting your business to be seen online is paramount to a successful business. It is no different then having a nice looking storefront for new customers to find you on a physical street, as it is to have that same customer locate you online. Having a quality website that is easy to find online is very important, just like having a business show in the Google 3 Pack would be in receiving new leads.

The quality of a businesses online presence can make or break financial success. Having a quality reputation online is paramount to success. Having a high ratings score is vitally important, but you must also have more actual reviews to stand above your competition. This should be a focus for all businesses. Lacking a high reputation score should never be taken lightly and sadly many small to mid sized business have never even looked at their score, or if they have, ignored the lower rating, because they do not know how to have a systematic approach to increasing their reputation.

This is why this book is written, to help share insight and knowledge with small to mid sized businesses on how and why a quality reputation score should be utilized to help increase new paying customers. Jim has been called the Google Ratings Guy because of his knowledge and expertise in helping businesses repair their online reputation and teaching how to get quality reviews in order to stand above your competition. But having great reviews does little if your business is not found with online searches. Having a quality website helps build your online presence and when created properly will deliver new leads through your business door.

Jim knows that businesses are loosing tens of thousands of dollars a year, because of their reputation score, and it is usually not indicative of the actual service provided. Jim believes that having a quality reputation score is the foundation of a solid lead generating system to help businesses grow to become successful. You can call Jim at the Up Your Rep Local (909) 541-5987 or visit UpYourRepLocal.com for more information.

What is online reputation management?

Online reputation management is really just managing a reputation online. For small business owners, it's the same as managing their reputation in their business. When a business owner hears that a customer is unhappy with their product or service, they may try to turn the unpleasant experience around right at the time of the instance, or they might reach out to them the next time the customer is in the store. By doing this, they're managing their reputation.

Managing a business' reputation online isn't much different. It involves finding out what consumers are saying, creating content that guides the conversation in a positive way, and addressing – when necessary – unpleasant or negative experiences.

Business owners can do this on their own simply by searching for their brand online, identifying problems, and creating solutions in the form of press releases and other content. But business owners are busy running their businesses, often too busy to be searching for their brand online.

For this, online reputation management consultants are available that can take over the sometimes menial and time-consuming tasks. Because these consultants can identify problems sooner, and know how to fix them when they occur, more and more businesses are starting to use them.

Why is online reputation management so important?

Business owners often ask this before they know what online reputation management. Once they do, and once they realize that they can take the "online" portion out of it, it becomes clear. It's managing your reputation, and that as a business owner, is extremely important. Even after business owners understand this though, they sometimes mistakenly think that because it is online, that it's not as important as their reputation out "in the real world." They couldn't be more wrong.

Imagine if you had an unhappy customer, holding up a sign outside your business that read "This business is bad" what would you do?

Probable do something to have the person stop, because everyone who sees the person, may think the message is true, that your business is bad. With Online messaging, it can be even worse, because the message can stay visible for a very long time.

What people are saying online today is everything, and it should *mean* everything to the business owner. Some might think that because they don't have an online business, their online reputation isn't important. That's wrong. Even when customers are going to visit a physical location to purchase the product or use a service, most people look online before they go. They see what people are saying, they take it into great consideration before deciding where or what to buy, and it greatly influences their future purchase.

This is why online reputation management is so important. Because even when business owners don't know it, people are out there talking about them. Those conversations, tweets, and reviews are making their way to the top of the search engines; so not only can other consumers see them, they might be the only things they see about a particular brand or business. If those conversations and reviews are negative, they can ruin a company whereas, if they're positive, they can significantly increase revenue for any business.

How can I find out what people are saying about my brand online?

Of course, once business owners realize that people are out there talking about them and their business, they want to find out what it is people are saying. The easiest way to do this is to start by searching for information on the company in the major search engines. Google, Yahoo and Bing are the biggest search engines, and the best ones to start any search on.

Business owners can start by searching for the company name and the names of products or services they offer. The terms that are used can then be used with "review" followed. This will provide search results on review sites such as Yelp and TripAdvisor. These reviews are often detailed and written by the customer, so business owners can see exactly what people are saying, and the experiences they had.

When searching for your own brand or business, it's important that you become anonymous. Google and the other major search engines have made such strides in optimizing searches during recent years that they track your history and provide results based on what you might be the most interested in.

While this is convenient for the average search, it's not when you're searching for reputation management purposes.

This is because you want to know what search results will appear when the average person searches for your business. In order to do this, you need to log out of any search engine accounts and turn off the personalized search option in the search engines.

When trying to find out what people are saying about your business, it's also important to look at the number one ranking in all the search engines. Is it your website? Is it a press release? Is it something you or your company created and published? If not, you may have your first problem with your online reputation.

What is a good review score vs. a bad review score?

A good review score is one that is either 4.7 – 4.9 with many reviews, or a score that is significantly better than your competitors. Some business seem to have a tendency to have more negative comments then positive comments. These services usually have their clients supplied to them through insurance referrals. Yes, many large medical practices seem to attract the negative reviews and do not seem to foster the positive reviews. Generally speaking here are my thoughts on review scores for the general local business.

4.7 – 5.0 Excellent

4.4 – 4.6 Great

4.0 – 4.3 Ok, but does not send confidence to consumers

3.7 – 3.9 Probably not going to visit there

3.5 – 3.6 Horrible Score

Under 3.5 May be time to pack it in!

A few bad reviews can really do damage, especially to a business that does not actively get many reviews from their customers. If you only Have 10 reviews, all 5.o and you get a new review with a 1 score, your perfect 5.o will drop to a 4.6 immediately. One more negative 1 score will drop you to a 4.3 score. So every single review can move your rating review score up or down very quickly.

Should I respond to negative reviews?

Whenever a business owner hears or sees that there's a bad review about them online, often the first thing they want to do is get online and respond to the review. Sometimes business owners can become so inflamed by a bad review, especially when it's untrue, that they want to attack the attacker.

This is *not* the way to respond to negative reviews. And in fact, in some cases, it's best not to respond to them at all. So how do you know when to respond, and when not to?

One of the key concepts in understanding this is to determine if the business was in the wrong, and if there's a solution to the problem. For example, a customer tries to use two coupons at a grocery store and is told by the cashier that they can only use one at a time. The customer goes online and writes a negative review, stating that they'd never been told about the policy before and has in fact used multiple coupons at once before at that location. Once the review is online, it's there for anyone to see. And if there's a solution, it may be appropriate to respond to the review.

The grocery store owner could reply to the review, apologizing for the cashier's mistake, explaining that they were in training and confused the store policy. Or, the grocery store owner could reply to the review, explaining that using multiple coupons was once allowed at the store, but the policy had been changed recently.

When replying to reviews, it's very important that an apology is always followed up with a solution, when possible. In this case it would most likely be a simple matter of refunding the customer for the coupon amount, or even sending them many coupons in the mail. A free item could also be offered to the customer the next time they're in the store. Any of these solutions would make the customer feel appreciated and listened to, and would help both the business and the business' online reputation.

When the business owner is not in the wrong, and there is no real solution, there is no need to reply to the review or complaint. This happens most often when a customer simply did not get what they want, regardless of the policy, and/or they simply wanted to defame the business online. It's unfortunate, but it does happen.

When it does, it's best just to let it lie. Not only will engaging with these customers start a war that there's really no way for the business owner to win, but the very start of that battle will make the business owner look bad in the eyes of other customers. Even worse, continuing an online debate only continues to push that review to the top of the search engine ranks. When the business owner lets the review go, the search engines will too and soon, it will get lost in the shuffle.

Can slander on social networking sites be taken down?

Social networking sites are a business owner's best friend, but they can also be their worst enemy. Social networking allows business owners to interact with their customers directly, often in a forum that the business owners control. But when a customer has posted a slanderous tweet, status update, or other form of comment or review that the business owner can't control, it can be difficult to get it taken down.

Unless the comment has violated the terms of service of the site, often the website will err on the side of the consumer. This is because these sites were designed with the intent of sharing information, and that includes among consumers. However, when the comments are outright abusive or can be shown to be slanderous and untrue, sometimes the commenter will be found in violation of the site's terms agreement, and the comment will be taken down.

Instead of focusing their efforts on having negative reviews or slander taken down, it's best for business owners to combat the problem with positive reviews and positive content that will overtake the negative.

Should I hire a lawyer?

If someone was to slander a business "in the real world," the first instinct the business owner might have is to hire a lawyer. And in the most persistent of cases, this might be a good idea. But it's never a good idea when the slander or negative comments are being made online.

Hiring a lawyer is an expensive process, not to mention a long one. By the time any real settlement or judgement is made, the slander would have gone away on its own online. And by continuing to bring attention and press to it, it will only keep the slander in the top search engine results longer. That means more people will be talking about it more often – the exact opposite of the desired result in this situation.

Other than waiting for negative reviews to fall out of the search engines, is there anything I can do to build a positive online reputation?

Yes! And in fact, the best way to combat negativity online is to create positivity. Business owners can do this in a number of ways.

One of the best ways is to create a process to collect positive reviews. Having negative reviews is not the end of the world, in fact it can be a good thing! Yes, you read me correctly, a good thing because having a perfect score (5.0) is generally looked upon as too good. Do you remember when you were in school, and the one student always got 100%. Everyone else in class wondered secretly if they were really that smart or cheated. Well, this is no different, you want an occasional negative remark to show that your business is legit. But if your score is below 4.0 then we definitely must be concerned. The best score is 4.7 – 4.9, and having a larger number of reviews over you competition is also a best practice. Let's say one of my competition has a 4.9 and 18 reviews. I want to get at least 4.8 and 119 reviews. That way people will say to themselves you know, a hundred more reviews means they are more legit and I trust that more.

Another great way to combat negative reviews is to create a website with top-notch content that includes not only promotional pages and material, but also helpful hints and tips and news about the industry. A good website, complete with keywords and SEO tactics is a business owner's number one defense against a negative online reputation. One great company we are associated with is the $249 Website Company, where they understand the issues of online reputation and offer solutions focused on helping the small to midsized business owner.

Create a blog. This is more content and more information that the search engines can pick up and place high in their search rankings. Even more importantly, it's information that the business owner controls, so it's all creating positivity. Blogs can be used to provide up to date information and current news.

Register the business with local online directories. Claiming the business name across all online directories has two purposes. The first is that it's yet another online location that the business owner can claim and that will help them get higher in the search engine rankings. It's also information that the business owner controls, which against helps create an online reputation. This is helpful because when customers can't find anything about a business online, they're apt not to trust it. Registering with online directories is also beneficial because if it's left open, someone else can claim it and use it to defame the business.

Create a profile across all social networking platforms. This will again, claim a space for the business high in the search engine results, and it also gives business owners a chance to directly interact with their customers.

Monitor social networks for mentions. Social media doesn't do business owners any good if they're not paying attention to what people are saying. It's important not only to blast the social network audience with information, but also interact with followers. Business owners need to pay special attention when they're directly mentioned by anyone on social media, and reply when they are.

Publish press releases. Press releases can be published and shared online very quickly. Creating a press release is an opportunity for business owners to tell their customers about major sales, new arrivals, and major news in the industry. And, just like all online content, press releases give the business owner one more place in the search rankings; and it's a place they control what's being said.

How can I create a positive online reputation when I'm busy running my business?

This is one of the biggest questions business owners have when they realize just how much time it can actually take to create, build, and protect an online reputation. And it's a valid one.

It's true that creating a positive online reputation does take time, and not only initially. Once a positive reputation has been established, it takes a constant effort to protect and maintain that reputation. And it's understandable that business owners just don't have the kind of time it takes to put in that work when they're busy running a great business. It's for this reason that more and more businesses are relying on online reputation management consultants.

These individuals spend their days scouring the web, creating profiles and gaining followers. They know how to find out what people are saying, and they know how to fix it when they find something negative. They know what positive content needs to be created to help the business place higher in the search engine rankings, and they can create it all.

The fees of a professional online reputation management consultant are minimal, but in today's online world, they're invaluable. Up Your Rep Local was created for this very purpose. To help the local business by providing the services at a very affordable fee. You can check them out at UpYourRepLocal.com.

Will an online reputation management consultant be able to eliminate all negative reviews online?

While consultants can be helpful, it's important that business owners remain realistic. While consultants are experts, they don't have total control over the actions of others. When consultants find negative reviews, they will send a request to the webmaster, asking them to remove the review with a brief explanation of why they're making the request. After the request is made, it is up to the discretion of the webmaster whether or not the review is removed. It is their website after all, and for the most part, they're allowed to put whatever they want on it.

What type of results will my business see with an online reputation management consultant?

Of course, no business owner wants to invest in something that's not going to give them results, but there's really no way to ever guarantee 100% accuracy with reputation management campaigns. The results will vary depending on the current state of the business' online reputation, how urgent the situation is, and how much new content needs to be created.

However, there are some things any business owner can expect out of a consultant. They should bring with them expert advice within the areas of brand and reputation management, they should report anything they find in a timely manner and sit down with the owner to decide how to deal with issues, and the business owner should be kept up to date at all times about the status of the project.

Can a consultant guarantee me a #1 spot in Google?

Page rankings and a business' online reputation go hand in hand, and to keep a positive reputation online, holding the #1 spot in Google's search results is a goal for any business owner. But, no business owner can guarantee a spot in #1, and neither can any consultant. In fact, Google themselves state that the number one spot cannot be guaranteed to anyone at any time, due to the fact that the algorithms are always changing and that spot is always in a state of flux.

But while business owners shouldn't hire a consultant expecting that they'll soon claim the top spot in Google, they should be wary of any consultant who guarantees such results – especially if they claim to have a priority or special relationship with Google. It simply isn't true. Getting into the Google 3-Pack is really what you want to achieve. Here a person can see the top three selections based on the search criteria entered into the Google search field.

But as we have noted earlier, Google has a habit of changing the algorithms on a regular basis. Just this July 2019, Google added a new filter requiring websites to be mobile optimized, and be fast or the algorithms will give you less of a ranking position score within their servers. Also, Google is beginning to utilize a new filter to reward websites who use SSL (Secure Sockets Layer) protection on their sites. In fact, if you do not have SSL (Secure Sockets Layer) your site may be blocked with a message that says warning, this site is not secure, proceed at your own risk! How's that for punishing those that do not necessarily need the SSL certificate, but will be punished with a strong warning most individual would avoid.

Therefore, keeping your eye on where you are currently ranking is vital for success.

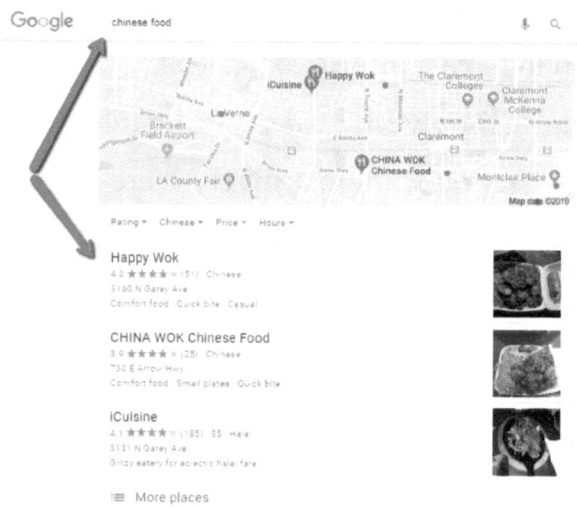

How much does it cost to invest in online reputation management?

Again, there is no one answer to this, and every case will be different. Spending the time to find out what consumers are saying about a particular brand or product online doesn't cost any more at all, and theoretically, a business owner could take care of most reputation management tasks on their own and with very little cost.

But in actuality, there is a cost attached. Even if the owner did it themselves, the cost there is still time – time that business owners don't typically have. Hiring a consultant can cost a business anywhere from $500 to $30,000, depending on how big their company is, and how much damage has already been done. There may also be small fees associated with things like online directories, which will help a business' online reputation in the end.

In most cases, online reputation management is a very affordable undertaking for most business owners, even when they hire the help of a consultant.

I know Up Your Rep Local is very affordable and many small business can set up service for as little as $50 a month. It may be worth checking out their services, before paying more to the other reputation management companies out there.

How long does it take for reputation management to work?

All businesses are unique, and so too are their online reputations. Because of this, there's really no way to tell how long a reputation management campaign will take for any one business, without knowing the full extent of their current online reputation. If a company has little to no online reputation when they hire a consultant, it can take as little as just a few weeks to build up that reputation. However, if there is a lot of slander or negative content out there about the business, it could take as long as a year.

Why does it take so long?

While managing an online reputation is important, it's definitely not something that happens overnight. One of the reasons why a campaign may take longer than a business owner was expecting is simply because there's a lot of work to be done on different websites. A consultant must visit all the different social media sites and set up profiles and pages for the business. Then they must also visit all the local online directories and claim the business on each of these, as well as set up a profile. The consultant may even have to set up a blog, or a website for the business.

All of these efforts are so that the content out there about the company is good, and more importantly, that it outweighs any negative content that may be out there. Putting in this kind of work simply takes time.

Another reason why it can take so long before business owners start seeing results from their online reputation campaign is because search engines don't rank new sites very high in the results. So if a blog or website is made, it's going to take time before the search engines give it a high ranking that's above negative content.

What role do search engines play in a person's or company's online reputation?

When a business owner thinks about their online reputation, it's natural to first think about the commenters or reviewers – those people who are actually out there, saying things about the company. But there's more to it than that. Because before a commenter's remark can be put online, the search engines need to decide where to place that remark within their own search rankings.

Search engines are like the gatekeepers of the internet. Using complex algorithms, they decide what content is most important and relevant to users, and will place content accordingly so in the results pages. When business owners start thinking like this, they realize just how large of a role search engines hold in online reputation campaigns, and just how important they are.

What are the main search engines that affect online reputations?

Long gone are the days of just having an option of one or two search engines. Today, people can find a search engine just about anywhere they look, and some are even specialized to specific industries or topics. But while all search engines will affect an online reputation to a degree, there are some that are bigger than others and as such, have more of an impact.

Think about it. If millions of people are using Google every day, that's potentially millions of people that could come across any one particular business. But if only thousands of people are using a smaller search engine, such as Dogpile, fewer people will have access to that one business. The same works for comments and reviews. When trying to fix or build an online reputation, it's important to start with the larger search engines and work down to the smaller ones.

So where does one start? Google is the main search engine, with the highest number of users. They have over 1 trillion pages in their index and they grow by the billions every day. Yahoo. Bing, Ask and AltaVista are the next biggest search engines after Google.

What are Google Direct Answers?

Google is trying to save users time in their search so, instead of forcing them to look through multiple websites before finding their search query, at times Google will provide a Direct Answers box. This box appears before all the other search results and gives a brief explanation or description of the searched term. This helps searchers immensely, but it can help business owners, too.

Business owners want to be seen as the expert in their industry, the authoritative voice on the matter. When a portion of their web page is displayed in a Google Direct Answers box, it only helps reinforce the idea that they are the leading voice on the matter. Also, in addition to the answer, Google also places a link back to the page where the answer was taken from, increasing how prominently sites appear in the search results, and the visibility those sites are given.

What is search engine optimization?

Of course, the search engines don't have actual people scouring the web every day, ranking pages and websites. This would be an impossible task. Instead they have little robot "spiders" that go out, look for key components of websites, and rank those sites accordingly in the search engine results. Because these spiders are electronic, users need to enter information that they'll understand and be able to identify. This is known as search engine optimization.

When you break down the phrase, search engine optimization is just optimizing – making the best use out of – a website so that it can be recognized by the search engines. There are a number of SEO tactics that reputation consultants, web hosts, and content developers use in order to make their sites seen by the search engines.

One of the biggest tactics is to use keywords throughout the site. These are the words users will enter into a search engine when they're looking for a specific topic; and they're one of the best SEO tactics that can be used. Links, either internally or to external sites, are another way that sites can be optimized so that they can be easily identified by the search engines.

Can I be notified when my company is mentioned online?

Of course, one of the tasks that requires the most time when building and managing an online reputation is trying to stay on top of what everyone is saying about the company, brand, product, or service. And not only does this need to be done at the very beginning of an online reputation campaign, it needs to be done regularly throughout the campaign; and it needs to be regularly done once the campaign is thought to be over, for the most part. Otherwise, those comments and reviews are just going to pile up again.

Thankfully, there's an easy way to do this. Business owners simply need to subscribe to Google Alerts, Social Mention, Brandwatch, or any other monitoring tools they think will be useful. These tools scour the web every single day and send an email notification to the business owner when the keyword (company's name or brand) is used. This gives the business owner a daily look into what users are saying about them and their company, and alerts them right away that there's a problem that may need to be fixed.

Are there other tools I can use to help me track my online reputation?

Only dozens! There are so many tools available to business owners that have been created with the sole intent of helping those business owners stay on top of their reputation and what people are saying about them. Yahoo Alerts works very similarly to Google Alerts, and Feedreader is also a great way to get entire articles that have been posted about the company or brand. Social Mention is a great way to see what people are saying across all social networking sites, while Twitter search and Facebook search are functions within social platforms that will help business owners make better use of them.

Of course, there are also all of the local online directories and the many different social media sites that business owners should be a part of. There are tons of tools designed specifically to help business owners track their online reputation, and all business owners should be using at least a few of them.

What social networking sites are the most important for my company?

This will largely depend on the company and the industry the company is in. And while some consultants may advise that every business be present on every social networking platform, this isn't necessary in all cases. For instance, YouTube videos get a very high ranking in the search engine results because it's such a huge website. YouTube is also owned by Google and helps Google rankings too. But it may not be appropriate for all businesses to have a YouTube channel. In some cases, it will simply be a matter of the business owner's discretion and where they want to appear.

There are some social networking sites however, that *all* businesses should be on. Facebook is the largest social networking site there is, so it's important that all business owners at least claim a page for their business, if not a personal profile. In addition, LinkedIn is known for being a social networking platform for professionals, and is to be used as a place for networking with other professionals in the industry and like-minded individuals. Because of this, every business should also have a LinkedIn company page.

And then there are the industry-specific social networking sites. These include platforms such as ActiveRain, a website designed to bring real estate agents, mortgage brokers, and others in the real estate market together. Avvo on the other hand, is a social networking site designed to connect lawyers with those seeking legal help and advice. When there are social networking sites such as these that are designed for specific industries, business owners in that industry should make it a point to be a member, and to be active, on those platforms.

Does my company website represent my business in the best possible way?

This is a question that most business owners don't think to ask, but they should. And most don't think to ask because they believe that their website does in fact represent their business in the best possible way. After all, they put a great deal of thought into it when they created it, they may have even hired professionals to help them maintain that website, and it says everything they want it to say.

All of this could be true, and the company's website still does not represent the business in the best possible way. Maybe it's simply straightforward basic information with little engaging content. Or perhaps it's missing information that the business owner didn't even think to include. The biggest mistake though, is often that the company's website URL doesn't directly mirror the actual business name, making it difficult for people (and search engines) to find it.

A company's website is their first defense when it comes to online reputations, and so during any branding campaign, the website must be looked at with a very critical eye.

How does my company's online reputation stack up to my competitors?

Business owners must always be aware of their competition, what they're doing, and how the business stacks up to those of offering the same product or service. This holds true when it comes to the competition's online reputation as well.

Searching for a competitor's name or product can be very helpful and will show business owners instantly what people are saying about their competition. Business owners should look at the top search results, if the results are positive or negative, and what exactly the piece of content is. This information will provide insight as to what the competition is doing right when it comes to their online reputation, and what they're getting wrong.

To learn who is your competitor, a business should type the search bar, service they provide followed by the city they are located. As an example, if I was a hair stylist in my city of La Verne, California. I would search hair salon La Verne, or Barber La Verne, maybe even Men's hair cut La Verne, any of these would show me who my competition is. It is also important to look a few long tail key words. If I was looking for auto mechanic, I may put auto repair, auto care, auto mechanic, car repair, care care, car mechanic to see each listing to see where I am listed against my completion, and to see what reputation score my competition has. Once you know, where you are in relation to your competition, will give you an idea of the reputation management ahead of you. If you are have a review reputation that may need some repair, then it is well worth the expense of time or money to get that taken care of.

Next Steps

Thank you reading this book. We hope that you found it useful and that it has given you the information you need to help you better understand the importance of managing your online reputation and the strategies to employ to help you do just that.

However, many people realize that the time and effort to build a better online reputation, would be better spent making money doing the business they love, or spending quality time with their family. If this is you, no problem, we can help!

We would love to help you build your online reputation to a place that can help bring in more profit for your business. Simply reach out to Jim at (909) 541-5987 or go to UpYourReplocal.com to get your free consultation set up.